AD ORIENTEM

AD ORIENTEM

The Direction that Changes Everything

PETER A. KWASNIEWSKI

TAN Books
Gastonia, North Carolina

Ad Orientem was first published by TAN Books as a chapter entitled "Why We Worship Facing East" within *Turned Around* (2024). Originally, two substantial portions of this chapter were published at *New Liturgical Movement* as "How Contrary Orientations Signify Contradictory Theologies" on November 5, 2018, and "Mass 'Facing the People' as Counter-Catechesis and Irreligion" on August 20, 2018.

Translations of the Bible used in this work are listed in the Bibliography

Cover design by Jordan Avery
Cover image: *Mass celebrated in ruined Church, Milan, Italy, WW1*. Mary Evans Picture Library/Robert Hunt Library / Bridgeman Images.

ISBN: 978-1-5051-4023-1
ePUB ISBN: 978-1-5051-4049-1

Published in the United States by
TAN Books
PO Box 269
Gastonia, NC 28053
www.TANBooks.com

Printed in India

Contents

Facing the Lord: The Meaning and Necessity of *Ad Orientem* Worship

The source and summit of our Christian life is the Eucharist, and the holy sacrifice of the Mass is the single greatest prayer that could ever be on earth. As St. John Henry Newman wrote, "Nothing is so consoling, so piercing, so thrilling, so overcoming, as the Mass, said as it is among us. I could attend Masses forever and not be tired. . . . It is not the invocation merely, but, if I dare use the word, the evocation of the Eternal."

For centuries, the Christian life was centered entirely on sacred worship, oriented to it as its goal. Towns and villages were built with churches and cathedrals at their center. The church bell's toll gave rhythm and structure to daily life. All things pointed to God, and all that Christian people did and lived for culminated in the sacrifice of the Mass. Yet, after nearly two millennia of such divine worship, the plague of modernity, of self-centered concerns, of lukewarm convictions, have infiltrated what was once held as sacred. We allowed the noise and dust of modern life to seep into the Mass and rearrange our worship, turning our gaze away from God and toward ourselves.

To Catholics familiar with the traditional Latin Mass, nothing is more sacred. To a person not familiar with the Latin Mass, nothing is perhaps more mystifying. "What's going on at the altar?" one asks. "Why is the priest turned away from me? I can't understand anything. I don't feel like I'm participating. I . . . me . . . I . . ." And such is the self-centered nature of the modern liturgy. What was once an ancient, sacramental liturgy and prayer focused entirely on Our Lord has become marred by our human tendency to turn all things back to ourselves, to water-down difficult or supernatural truths, to pad our fragile egos in order to feel we are indeed special and faultlessly worthy of approaching God in any way we desire.

The Mass is both deeply familiar and mystically elusive for many Catholics. We know its rhythms, its responses, its seasons; we know when to sit, stand, and kneel; we recite the prayers and try to align our hearts and minds toward God. And yet, for all this familiarity (especially with the modern liturgy's express intention of making the Mass more familiar and inclusive), the beauty and truth of the Mass remains far above human understanding. What, precisely, is happening here? To whom is it directed? What is unfolding when a priest ascends the altar and begins to pray?

Such questions used to be answered in the ceremonies of the liturgy itself, an explanation evident in posture, instinct, and perception. With the introduction of the *Novus Ordo* liturgy, this silent catechesis went away.

Symbols and gestures were abandoned, emptied, or inverted. Reverence toward God took second chair to the human desire for community, for feeling comfortable and included. What was once a true community of faithful, all oriented toward Our Lord, all together raising one Eucharistic hymn, was exchanged for ditties, socials, and homilies linked to NFL games and TV shows.

Long before the Gospel is preached or a hymn resounds, the arrangement of a sanctuary and the bodily orientation of those within it *already proclaim a theology*. One need not be a scholar or even a believer to sense this. Anyone who has stepped into a Catholic church, watched a congregation kneel in unison before the Blessed Sacrament, or felt the gravity of silence settle at the words of the consecration, knows that something important is being said without words.

Since the Second Vatican Council in the 1960s and especially in recent decades, much attention has been given to the spoken content of the Mass: its language, its accessibility, its explanatory clarity. Far less attention has been paid to the more primordial language of the body—the language of how we stand, where we look, what we collectively face. Yet human beings are not disembodied minds. We learn first through our senses. We intuit meaning through movement and orientation long before we articulate it conceptually. In worship especially, the body often grasps what the intellect struggles to name. This is why even small changes in ritual posture can have far-reaching effects, not merely aesthetic but spiritual and doctrinal.

This booklet is concerned with one such significant change in the liturgy: the direction of prayer in the celebration of the Mass. At first glance, the question may appear trivial or even falsely pious. But appearances can deceive. As we shall see, the orientation of the priest and people is not a decorative detail layered onto the liturgy from without; it is one of the ways the liturgy reveals its inner truth. To ask *which way do we face?* is, ultimately, to ask *toward whom we are turned?* And in the answer to that question lies a great deal more than one might expect—nothing less, in fact, than the difference between a worship that opens the soul toward God and one that quietly, almost imperceptibly, folds it back in on itself.

Why We Worship Facing East

Catholics who delve into serious discussions of liturgy, wishing perhaps to know what all the fuss is about, quickly discover that one of the hottest of hot-button questions is the orientation of the liturgy. Msgr. Klaus Gamber once claimed that turning the altar and priest around to face the people was the single most destructive change that occurred in the celebration of the Mass (and he was not favorable to most of the other changes either). What *is* the big deal, then, about the direction the priest is facing at Mass?[1]

I would like to begin with two testimonials. Both are taken, on purpose, from Catholics who would not call themselves "traditionalists." To my mind, this gives their perspectives more weight, inasmuch as they cannot be accused of wanting to "turn the clock back." Their views are based simply on how things appear to them. The first is from a layman, David Clayton, the impresario of Pontifex online university and the author of many books and articles on "the Way of Beauty,"

---

[1] This topic has been taken up many times at the website *New Liturgical Movement* (hereafter "*NLM*"), but there are always more angles from which to pursue it, and we will never leave it alone. Those who wish to read more should search *NLM* with the keyword "ad orientem."

who says the following about his experience of worship facing eastwards:

> This is perhaps the most striking and immediate way of symbolizing that we look to and recognize a Higher Power. My own conversion was influenced by seeing an *ad orientem* Mass in which the priest was seen as the head of a body of people, leading us towards a common destination. This impression just described was accentuated by the architecture and art [of the church—the Brompton Oratory in London], which served to focus my attention on and present to me visually images of what I otherwise would not have intuited.[2]

A diocesan priest, Fr. Dwight Longenecker, wrote some years ago about offering Mass *ad orientem* or toward the east:

> I celebrate facing the same way as the people because I actually feel closer to them that way. I also feel closer to God. When I . . . face the Lord with the people I find that my own celebration of Mass is more intimate and mystical. I feel like I am able to focus more on the Lord and what is happening. If I need to weep I can do so without people seeing

[2] Clayton, "Connecting *Ad Orientem*, Sacred Art, an Ordered Environmentalism, Social Graces, and a Hierarchical Society."

> me. If I need to pause and pray I can do so without worrying what people are thinking.[3]

He then comments on one particular experience that he believes was made possible for him, in part, by the fact that he was not, so to speak, "on display," but focused on the prayer, with nothing before his eyes except the missal, the altar, and the holy oblations:

> As I celebrated Mass a strange awareness came over me. As I read the words from the missal it was as if the words themselves were alive and vivid. I cannot explain what I was seeing except to say that the words were thronged with the meaning of the words. The words on the page were distinct and that made every doctrine and truth distinct. It was as if each word and even each letter stood out with cosmic significance—not that the words themselves were so alive, but that the eternal meaning and truths that the words communicated were alive and throbbing with the meaning—meaning that was alive as far above me as the stars, and as close to me as my own breath. Then I thought of the mysterious meaning of "In the beginning was the Word and the Word was with God and the Word was God…and the Word became flesh and dwelt

[3] Longenecker, "From a Priest at the Altar."

> among us." It was as if this eternal mystery of the Incarnation was coming true again within the simple speaking of the words. Something happened. A transaction was made between this world and eternity.

Now, the way things appeared to Mr. Clayton and Fr. Longenecker is, I maintain, the way in which they naturally appear, or have the potential to appear, to anyone who arrives on the scene without prejudices.

Imagine a person with no knowledge of the Catholic Faith or perhaps even of Christianity deciding, out of curiosity, to step from a bright sunlit street into an attractive Catholic church or chapel. As his eyes adjust, he sees a number of faithful dotted here and there in the pews, kneeling and looking ahead. At the far end of the church, in a more open area with more decoration than the rest of the building, he sees a group of men, dressed in strange and elaborate garb, clustered round a large marble object with candles across it. They are all facing the same direction as the faithful in the church; they are intensely focused on what they are doing; their bodies block his view of their work,[4] but they look for

[4] How often have we heard, as an objection to *ad orientem:* "The people should be able to *see* what's going on"? Those who say that must never have read *The Little Prince,* which transmits the wisdom of mankind: *"On ne voit bien qu'avec le coeur. L'essentiel est invisible pour les yeux"* (Saint-Exupéry, *Le Petit Prince,* 76: "You can see well only with your heart. What is essential is invisible to the eye"). No

all the world as if they might be huddling around a sacrificial victim to kill it. It is clear, at any rate, that their attention is *not* focused on the people. Our observer feels that something very solemn and serious is happening, and that everyone in the building is, in their different ways, utterly united in this action, whatever it may be. If, in addition, our hypothetical visitor hears chant or polyphony, and smells incense, and feels the hard wood against his legs, worn smooth by so many worshipers over the years, four of his outward senses will be, like the four evangelists, proclaiming a presence to him, even if he is not yet able to recognize it or call it by name.

Clayton speaks in a very similar way about that first Mass he attended at the Brompton Oratory:

> I couldn't understand the words. The three priests, one central and two flanking, each in ornately embroidered vestments, and the acolytes in white cotton had their backs to me and were facing towards the east (*ad orientem*), towards the giant altar. All the congregation faced east too, bowing, kneeling, standing and sitting together; and the priests seemed to be directing a common focus beyond

---

one can *see* the miracle of transubstantiation. What we *can* see are the sacramental signs of the Lord's presence—and *those* are shown to everyone in the elevation of the host and, less directly, the elevation of the chalice.

> themselves towards something mysterious. While I could not tell precisely what it was, they acted in unison, and so their body language spoke to me of their faith. They believed that what they were doing was of profound importance, I could tell. The mystery as to what that was in some way cleared, but in others intensified, when the priest held the white host aloft. I did not really know what I was seeing, but, nevertheless, my instincts told me powerfully that this was the focus of everything that had preceded it.... At that point I was only vaguely aware of what this [beauty of the integrated whole of this spectacle] was telling me, but I knew at a deep unspoken level, however dimly, that I was grasping a profound truth communicated to me by music, art, architecture, and body language.[5]

A visitor to such a liturgy has already begun to receive the first and most important lesson in the Christian religion: that *God* is the center of our attention, the goal of our strivings, the purpose of our lives. This visitor is seeing played out before him the meaning of Psalm 144:15: "The eyes of all hope in thee, O Lord: and thou givest them meat in due season." We have here a representation—and with it, the possibility of an experience—of man turning himself toward the source of his

---

5 Clayton, *The Way of Beauty*, 14.

being and destiny: as the old prayer says, "I acknowledge Thee to be my Creator and sovereign Lord." Nothing—no amount of catechesis or homiletics or pastoral programs—can ever substitute for this experience or even vie with it. Without this immediate and wordless awareness of God as the *mysterium tremendum et fascinans*, the fearful and fascinating mystery for whose sake we stop paying attention for a moment to each other and to this world and stumble up to the edge of His domain, where His presence may infiltrate and permeate *our* domain . . . without this, I say, there is no religion at all, no worship, no sacred liturgy. Without it, a liturgy may technically still happen, but the terrible words of the prophet Isaiah, cited by Our Lord, would then seem to fit the case: "This people honoureth me with their lips: but their heart is far from me. And in vain do they worship me, teaching doctrines and commandments of men."[6] The new forms of Catholic worship that came in after the Second Vatican Council so readily lend themselves to endless verbalization and explanation that they leave no place for Newman's *cor ad cor loquitur*, "heart speaks to heart." "This people honoureth me with their lips: but their heart is far from me"; and why? Because the minds of all are captured by a swirling anthropocentric vortex animated by "the doctrines and commandments of *men*,"[7] that is, the false philosophical

6 Matt. 15:8–9.

7 Matt. 15:9, emphasis added.

principles that guided the process by which we arrived at such novelties as *versus populum* (facing the people), with the church reconfigured as a closed circle presided over by a sort of clerical chairman.

Historical Foundations

To avoid any risk of worshiping the Most Holy Trinity in vain, let us try to discover the deepest reasons for the ancient and, until recently, uninterrupted custom of praying eastwards—a custom that we find from the East to the West, in every traditional rite of Christian worship, be it Byzantine or Latin; Slavic or Greek; Roman, Gallican, Ambrosian, or Mozarabic; Chaldean, Coptic, Armenian, or Ethiopian.

For starters, the custom of all Christians either offering or participating in the Eucharistic liturgy facing east has the same apostolic roots and the same universality in Church history as the use of water baptism, the praying of the Psalms, the worship of the risen Christ on Sunday, the honoring of the Mother of God and the saints, and the veneration of their relics. As a matter of fact, eastward orientation *predates* the use of official priestly vestments, consecrated church buildings, and the very Niceno-Constantinopolitan Creed that we recite every Sunday.[8] Does that make it old enough and

[8] The archaeological and documentary evidence for this claim is overwhelming: early Christians built (and understood themselves to be building) real and proper altars, not merely "tables," and they prioritized facing eastwards to offer the sacrifice. The evidence has been painstakingly compiled and analyzed in Heid, *Altar and Church*. It is

widespread enough to take seriously? If not, why do we take any of these other things seriously? They should be just as dispensable.

Think of it this way: Would you, if you are a practicing Catholic, want the Lord's Day to be abolished, replaced by another day of the week, or simply taken off the roster? That would be an unthinkable deviation from Christian practice. Would you want all the Psalms removed from the Mass and the Divine Office? Should we replace water baptism with a civil naming ceremony, or stop honoring our Blessed Mother because it might make us feel like immature children or offend anti-maternal feminists? Should priests celebrate Mass in jeans and T-shirts because that's the common clothing of our day, as robes and cloaks were the common clothing of ancient times? Impossible! It cannot be that

---

therefore of only marginal interest to note that some churches, owing to peculiar circumstances, were so situated that the altar had to be placed at the western end and the celebrant had to face the nave and thus the congregation; for he did so *in order* to face eastward. He was only incidentally standing "toward the people." Such anomalies show that, even where topography forced alternative designs, *ad orientem* remained a priority. Once the principle of a general unified orientation within a church (i.e., everyone facing the same way toward the apse) gained absolute precedence in church design, the literal or cosmic east was sometimes passed over in favor of the "liturgical east," i.e., *versus apsidem.* It is nevertheless far from ideal to sever the direction of the building from its cosmic framework, and every effort should be made to keep the architectural orientation in line with the cosmic orientation that is its foundation.

something we have done for millennia should suddenly be dropped. But this is exactly what has been done with *ad orientem* worship.

For nearly 2,000 years, clergy and faithful together faced the same direction in expectation of Christ and in adoration of Him, the One who already comes in mystery in the Most Holy Eucharist, the One who is to come manifestly at the end of the world to judge the living and the dead and the world by fire. *Ad orientem* preserves the eschatological orientation of the liturgy. When Christians first gathered on Sundays to worship the Lord, they were anticipating the second coming of Christ—this seems to be the oldest characteristic of our corporate worship. The "primordial form" of Sunday was not so much a feast looking back to the resurrection of Christ on the first Easter, or to any particular mystery or moment of His earthly life, as it was a looking *forward* with longing to the Lord's return in glory, imploring Him to deliver us from the evils of sin, death, and hell.[9] Sunday Mass was about *the life of the world to come*, which the early Christians, suffering bitter and horrific trials, must have thought about a great deal as they hoped and prayed that they would remain faithful: "lead us not into temptation but deliver us from evil."[10] For this reason, the eastward focus of prayer was a poignant symbol: after the dark and cold night, the

9 Dix, *The Shape of the Liturgy*, 336–37, 359–60, 368.

10 See Oppenheimer, "Towards the Second Coming."

sun will rise gloriously on the eastern horizon, shedding light and warmth.

This mindset found both inspiration and confirmation in the Scripture passages that call Christ "the Orient" or say that He ascends to the east, or that He will come from the east. For example, Jesus says of Himself, in Matthew 24:27: "As lightning cometh out of the east, and appeareth even into the west: so shall the coming of the Son of man be."[11] The prophet Zechariah announces the Messiah in this way: "Behold a man, the Orient is his name."[12] The prophet Malachi calls Christ "the Sun of justice."[13] The canticle of Zechariah, sung every day in Lauds, describes the Messiah as "*Oriens ex alto*," the "dawn . . . from on high."[14] God is called "Light" in John 1:5, and later in verse nine, His Son is called "the true light, which enlighteneth every man that cometh into this world," as indeed the physical sun does.[15] Implicit in the description of King Solomon's dedication of the first temple is an *ad orientem* priestly gesture: "And Solomon stood before the altar of the Lord in the sight of the assembly of Israel, and spread

---

[11] cf. Acts 1:10–11.

[12] Zach. 6:12.

[13] Mal. 4:2.

[14] Lk 1:78 RSVCE. Or, in the Douay-Rheims, with its customary literalism: "Through the bowels of the mercy of our God, in which the Orient from on high hath visited us."

[15] All these texts and more, with good commentary, may be found in the article by Hayden, "*Convertere, Israël, ad Dominum Deum Tuum!*"

forth his hands towards heaven."[16] This verse puts us in mind of the "Sursum corda" in the Preface dialogue, when the priest raises up his arms to God, gesturing that we should lift our hearts on high, to Him who lives and reigns forever, enthroned above the cherubim. The Divine Liturgy of St. John Chrysostom features a still more extroverted gesture, as the priest repeatedly bows and lifts his hands aloft during the Cherubikon or cherubic hymn.

Verses and practices like these were repeatedly commented on by the Church Fathers, such as St. Basil the Great (330–379), defender of the divinity of the third Person of the Blessed Trinity, and St. John Damascene (c. 675–c. 749), defender of icons. One of the most famous passages on our subject comes, in fact, from Basil's treatise *On the Holy Spirit*, published in the year 375. The Cappadocian father writes:

> Of the beliefs and practices whether generally accepted or publicly enjoined which are preserved in the Church, some we possess derived from written teaching; others we have received delivered to us "in a mystery" by the tradition of the apostles; and both of these in relation to true religion have the same force. And these no one will gainsay—no one, at all events, who is even moderately versed in the institutions of the Church. For were we to

16 1 Kgs 8:22.

> attempt to reject such customs as have no written authority, on the ground that the importance they possess is small, we should unintentionally injure the Gospel in its very vitals.

Basil then offers a lengthy list of beliefs and practices not contained verbatim in Scripture but handed down by tradition:

> What writing has taught us to turn to the East at the prayer?[17] Which of the saints has left us in writing the words of the invocation at the displaying of the bread of the Eucharist and the cup of blessing? For we are not, as is well known, content with what the apostle or the Gospel has recorded, but both in preface and conclusion we add other words as being of great importance to the validity of the ministry, and these we derive from unwritten teaching. We all look to the East at our prayers, but few of us know that we are seeking our own old country, Paradise, which God planted in Eden in the East.[18]

He then argues—bear in mind that this is a treatise in defense of the divinity of the third Person of the Trinity against those who deny it—that there is no more reason

---

[17] "The prayer" in the sense of the greatest prayer: the Eucharistic offering.

[18] Basil, *On the Holy Spirit,* 27:66.

to worship eastwards than there is to worship the Spirit, since *both* are handed down by tradition. But since we all agree about worshiping eastwards, we should likewise all adore the Holy Spirit as God! How is it possible for us to ignore the force of such a witness from the early Church? One is reminded of a similar argumentative move in St. Cyril of Alexandria's defense of the oneness of Christ, true God and true man, against Nestorius: we all know that the Holy Eucharist was given in order to divinize us; but if Christ is not truly the Son of God, receiving Him in Communion would never give us a share in the divinity; hence, He must be the Son of God. In arguing that way, Cyril, who died in 444, takes for granted a universal belief in the Real Presence of Christ in the Eucharist and deduces the divinity of Christ from it! Such examples are extremely embarrassing for Protestants, it must be admitted; but they are, sadly, no less embarrassing for modern Catholics, who seem only too willing to turn their backs on tradition—even when it can lay claim to apostolic origins.

Later, St. John Damascene ably summarized this particular tradition:

> It is not without reason or by chance that we worship toward the east. . . . Since God is spiritual light and Christ in sacred Scripture is called "Sun of Justice" (Mal 4:2) and "Orient" (Lk 1:78), the east should be dedicated to His worship Also, the divine David says: "Sing to God, ye kingdoms of

the earth: sing ye to the Lord; who mounteth above the heaven of heavens, to the east" (Ps 67:33f.). And still again, Scripture says: "And the Lord has planted a paradise in Eden to the east; wherein He placed man whom He had formed," and whom He cast out, when he had transgressed, "and made him to live over against the paradise of pleasure" (Gn 2:8; 3,24 LXX), or in the west. Thus it is that, when we worship God, we long for our ancient fatherland and gaze toward it.

As a matter of fact, when the Lord was crucified, He looked toward the west, and so we worship gazing toward Him. And when he was taken up, He ascended to the east and thus the Apostles worshiped Him and thus He shall come in the same way as they had seen Him going into heaven (cf. Ac 1:11), as the Lord Himself said: "As lightning cometh out of the east and appeareth even into the west: so shall also the coming of the Son of man be" (Mt 24:27). And so, while we are awaiting Him, we worship toward the east. This is, moreover, the unwritten tradition of the Apostles, for they have handed many things down to us unwritten.[19]

19 John Damascene, *De fide orthodoxa* 85 (IV 12), in *Writings,* 352–54.

The 180-degree turn in the stance of the priest—let's not forget that colloquially, someone who "does a 180" is someone who suddenly and completely changes his mind or course of action, implying a rejection of what came before—decisively severs us from that which is most ancient, most intrinsic, and most distinctive in our worship as Christians. Whenever people return to *ad orientem* worship, they return decisively to the fundamentals of Christian faith and its original practice. Ironically, in adopting the novelty of *versus populum*—a supposed "return to the earliest practice" in the judgment of (some) mid-twentieth century scholars, whose conclusions have been overturned by the work of subsequent scholars—*we ended up losing one of the most ancient elements of all.*[20]

---

[20] It is interesting to note that Fr. Joseph Jungmann, otherwise so influential in the liturgical reform, strongly defended the *ad orientem* posture. See his book (outdated in many ways) *The Early Liturgy to the Time of Gregory the Great,* 133–39. Similarly, although he expressed many criticisms of the Tridentine rite, Fr. Louis Bouyer staunchly defended the *ad orientem* stance in such works as *Rite and Man* and *Liturgy and Architecture.*

The Theological Meaning

It is not hard to see why this custom should have been nearly convertible with Christian worship as such—above all in the Mass, the highest act of worship. The Mass is both Patricentric and Christocentric: these are different but complementary perspectives. Because Christ is both Head of the Church *and* our God, one in His divinity with the Father and the Holy Spirit, we can be at one and the same time on our way *with Him* to the Father in the power of the Spirit, and on our way *to Him* as our ultimate end. It is therefore correct to say that the priest, praying *ad orientem*, is facing Christ (the Orient), and to say that he is praying, as *alter Christus* or *in persona Christi*, toward the Father. In fact, the clear symbolic proclamation of the twofold mystery of Christ as both our God and our mediator with God is completely lost in the *versus populum* stance. To face Christ, and to face the Father with Christ, are mutually implicated, just as they are in Scripture: "You call me Master, and Lord; and you say well, for so I am"; "I and the Father are one"; "he that seeth me seeth the Father also"; "I go to the Father: for the Father is greater than I."[21]

[21] John 13:13; 10:30; 14:9; 14:28.

Most simply, worship is about *God*, not about us. Or rather, it is about us only insofar as we are *from* God, *in* God, and *for* God, our Creator, Savior, Sanctifier, and Judge. Hence, even to the extent that, as St. Thomas Aquinas says, the liturgy is for our needs, since God who is infinitely good stands in need of nothing for Himself, it is still done for the love and praise and thanking *of God*, who is the source and fulfillment of our needs.[22] Our need, in short, is for *God*; our deepest need is to go beyond ourselves into Him. True worship takes us out of ourselves and establishes us in God, our ultimate end. In this sense, any aspect of liturgy that does not clearly terminate in God, Father, Son, and Holy Spirit, or any aspect that seems to terminate in *us*, is not liturgy, whatever else it may be (self-regard, social posturing, therapy, superstition).

Hence, the *ad orientem* stance simply expresses the act of worship as such, whereas the *versus populum* stance contradicts it outright. This is why the latter is not merely unfitting for worship but antithetical to the virtue of religion that adores God as first beginning

---

22 *Summa Theologiæ* II–II, Q. 81, art. 7: "We pay God honor and reverence, not for His sake (because He is of Himself full of glory to which no creature can add anything), but for our own sake, because by the very fact that we revere and honor God, our mind is subjected to Him; wherein its perfection consists, since a thing is perfected by being subjected to its superior, for instance the body is perfected by being quickened by the soul, and the air by being enlightened by the sun."

and last end. The theologian Max Thurian, writing (somewhat surprisingly) in the official Vatican journal *Notitiae*, observed: "The whole celebration [of Mass] is often conducted as if it were a conversation and dialogue in which there is no longer room for adoration, contemplation, and silence. The fact that the celebrants and faithful constantly face each other closes the liturgy in on itself."[23] This observation anticipated Joseph Ratzinger's similar and more famous remark in *The Spirit of the Liturgy*: "The turning of the priest toward the people has turned the community into a self-enclosed circle. In its outward form, it no longer opens out on what lies ahead and above, but is closed in on itself."[24] Along the same lines, the former papal master of ceremonies Guido Marini remarked at a conference in Rome:

> In our time, the expression "celebrating facing the people" has entered our common vocabulary. Such an expression would be categorically unacceptable the moment it comes to express a theological proposition. Theologically speaking, the holy Mass, as a matter of fact, is always addressed to God through Christ our Lord, and it would be a grievous error to imagine that the principal orientation of the sacrificial action is the community. Such an orientation,

---

[23] Thurian, "La Liturgie, contemplation du mystère," 2.

[24] Ratzinger, *Spirit of the Liturgy*, II.3, in *Theology of the Liturgy*, 49.

> therefore, of turning towards the Lord must animate the interior participation of each individual during the liturgy. It is likewise equally important that this orientation be quite visible in the liturgical sign as well.[25]

Marini helps us to see not only that the object of liturgy should always be God, or the God-man Jesus Christ, never mere man, but also that this objective *orient*ation (we cannot avoid the east even in our ordinary way of speaking!) should be *visible*, evident to the senses, easily grasped by the intellect, and easily translated into the movement of the will that we call love, which is ordered to the good—to a good outside of ourselves, in the case of our ultimate end.

The contrast between the postures can be articulated in terms of their subject/object signification. In the *ad orientem* arrangement, the subject/object appears as man/god. The priest both looks and acts like an image of Christ, the mediator between God and man, Himself always oriented to the Father.[26] Paradoxically, the ceremonial centrality of the priest in the old rite serves to emphasize that God is the one and only object of worship, since the priest is so obviously assimilated to

---

25 Marini, "Clergy Conference in Rome: Address of Msgr. Guido Marini, Papal Master of Ceremonies."

26 See Kwasniewski, "The Sacrifice of Praise and the Ecstatic Orientation of Man."

his office as *alter Christus*, as the head of a people on pilgrimage to the Kingdom of Heaven.

In the *versus populum* arrangement, the subject/object appears as people/ priest. The priest, even with the best of intentions and behavior, looks and acts like an empowered facilitator of a communal event; the *vis-à-vis* positioning confers on him a sort of autocratic prominence as the one to whom the congregation is subordinated and beholden. This may be the psychological reason why some priests overcompensate with informality, jokes, banter, smiles, waves, applause, or what have you—the priest's very "over-againstness" in *versus populum* seems to demand a downplaying of the over-against by means of emphasizing that he's really "one of us" after all! How sad that the one true and obvious way of representing that the priest is "one of us"— namely, by having him face in the same direction as everyone else and offer the sacrifice on their behalf, the very same sacrifice they are offering in their hearts—has been discarded as an opaque and expired symbol, to be replaced by a format that turns the Mass into something done *toward* the people and, in a sense, imposed upon them. In reality, the Mass is something Jesus Christ, according to His human nature, does toward the Most Holy Trinity, as the great prayer "Suscipe, sancta Trinitas" in the traditional Offertory perfectly expresses—and we are permitted to join in. Ironically, for a rite that is supposed to be less clericocentric and more congregational, the priest in the new rite becomes far more central and attention-getting because his personality, his "vernacular style" or "way of being a priest," intrudes. *Versus populum* does nothing but underline this unfortunate amplification of human presidency, undermining assimilation to Christ's *kenosis* or self-empyting and diluting His unique mediation.

When I was teaching in Wyoming, I often engaged my college students in conversation about liturgical matters and enjoyed listening to their spontaneous ideas. Most of them had never picked up a book about liturgy, but they intuitively understood a lot, simply from reflecting on their experiences. One student, a senior, decided to send me an email one day:

> The more I think about it, the more significant the *ad orientem* debate seems to me. Praying eastwards just *makes sense*. All of a sudden, the priest's personality *doesn't matter.* It seems like such a small thing, but I am convinced that if priests didn't face "the audience," they would act *and perceive themselves* very differently. Why? Because they are human. And humans love feeling powerful, like rock stars. The priest has become a performer, and that has enormous implications. Not only has his importance eclipsed that of the Eucharist in the eyes of the everyday Catholic, but I think this is a fundamental reason the priesthood started attracting the wrong kind of man. Before, the priest was an

> instrument, a mediator; someone who sacrificed his life for Christ in the Eucharist and for His bride the Church. Now the role of priest is the opposite of humble. He's a guru, a prophet, a philosopher and psychologist, a rock star, the host of a show. Before, he was a man with a job; now he's *someone.* Praying *ad orientem* entails an immediate shift in consciousness—and it would have the fringe benefit of turning off seminarians who are attracted for the wrong reasons. I know it's not the only reason the role of priest has been completely changed, but I think it might be one of the most basic.[27]

The phrase "seminarians who are attracted for the wrong reasons" is a delicate reference to the problem of clerical homosexuality.[28] For, beyond the temptation to pride, there is also an inherent effeminacy to *versus populum.* Based on Manfred Hauke's discussion of the sexes,[29] one can associate the symbol for the male (♂), an arrow shooting out from a circle, with *ad orientem*, and the symbol for the female (♀), a statically mounted circle, with *versus populum.* The eastward-oriented priest looks outward and leads the people as their head, directing them to the divine beyond creation;

[27] Private correspondence.

[28] See Francis Magister, "What Attracts Homosexuals to the Priesthood?"

[29] See Hauke, *Women in the Priesthood?*

the woman shelters, cradles, turns to the child, in an anthropological symbol of immanence, of rootedness in the created order. Due to the sacramental principle at work, the symbolic stance of the celebrant *effects a disposition*, a mentality, like that which it symbolizes. What is proper to a woman and a most beautiful perfection of hers becomes, in a priest or in men generally, effeminacy. The "mothering" of the congregation—particularly when it is done with a lecturey schoolmarm spirit—is deeply corrosive of spiritual virility. That is why Cardinal Heenan, as part of the group of bishops who were given a "sneak peak" of the Novus Ordo at the Synod of Bishops in 1967, predicted that the new rite would empty the churches of men; and it is no surprise that statistics show a much higher percentage of men in old-rite congregations today (sometimes more than 50%) than in new-rite ones.[30]

Kathleen Pluth brilliantly captures the problem and the solution. Having said that she hates being a cause of distraction to others by cantoring in the front of a church and that she much prefers the anonymity of the choir loft (singers should be heard and not seen), she then speaks about the celebrant of the Mass:

> The role of the priest is exponentially more complex. He cannot hide. His role is inherently, and in some regards primarily, visible, leading the con-

[30] For an extended reflection on these issues, see Shaw, *The Liturgy, the Family, and the Crisis of Modernity*, 215–72.

gregation through the veil, into the Holy of Holies. We follow him, as he expresses in the highest possible way his conformity to Jesus, our advocate before the Father. For centuries the symbolism of our "following" the priest was clear. However, in the postconciliar period, and without a direct referrent in the Council's documents themselves, the character of the priest's relationship to the people has been visibly distorted by the *versus populum* posture.

When people face each other, they aim to please. They make eye contact; they smile encouragingly. There is a word for such gestures: flattery. People flatter their priests and their priests flatter them, at an average ratio of, say, 500 to 1. None of this is encouraged in the Council documents. The *versus populum* posture is specifically worldly. It sets up the priest, not as a model to follow, but as a talk show host to be flattered insofar as he delights us. There are no good reasons for this.

The lines of sight to God should be made clear in the Liturgy (see Pseudo-Dionysius' *Ecclesiastical Hierarchy* for a beautiful exposition of how this should work), but instead our path towards God is obscured by the distracting cycle of eye-contact and feedback. The Sunday liturgy is for everyone their primary and for many their only contact with the Church. As such, its symbols should express the truth, including the truth about ecclesial relationships, which should not be a matter of flattery but of service. The Psalmist sings, "Let your priests be clothed with holiness/The faithful shall ring out their joy." The *ad orientem* posture lets priests be priests and [lets] the people be themselves too, all facing God together.[31]

[31] Pluth, "The First Step in Ecclesiastical Reform: Turn the Altars Around."

Of Divine and Diabolic Symbols

Accordingly, it was much to the devil's advantage to turn the priest around to the people, creating a charmed circle of neighborly affirmation that brought the experience of the Mass down to the level of a horizontal exchange, a back-and-forth in everyday speech. There is nothing transcendent about that; on the contrary, God is domesticated, tamed, manipulable—not a recipient of sacrifice but a subject of conversation. The liturgy comes to be *about* God instead of *for* Him. Indeed, as Ratzinger said, at times one wonders if there is any room left for God at all.[32] Reflecting on the symbolism of east and west at work in the Byzantine rite of baptism, David Clayton remarks:

> At one point we all turned as directed by our pastor to the west, in order to renounce Satan loudly and to make the gesture of spitting on him. We then turned around and to the east, *ad orientem*. This

[32] Ratzinger, *Milestones,* 148–49: "I am convinced that the crisis in the Church that we are experiencing today is to a large extent due to the disintegration of the liturgy, which at times has even come to be conceived of *etsi Deus non daretur,* in that it is a matter of indifference whether or not God exists and whether or not he speaks to us and hears us."

> was as much, it seemed to me, to turn our backs on Satan as to look for the Risen Christ. It was a powerful moment. Perhaps the same neglect [of piety in venerating holy images] opened the west door of the Church and left it ajar and unattended, drawing the "smoke of Satan" into the vacuum created by the absence of fragrant incense, followed (who knows?) by the entrance of Satan himself. If he did enter, he would likely not be greeted by a shower of spittle, but greeted in a spirit of diversity by a priest facing him directly, worshiping and making a sacrifice. What sort of message does that communicate, I wonder? Those who do realize the seriousness of what is going on and object to it are too often showered with spite, if not spittle, for their troubles.[33]

In the Western context, moreover, where the use of a sacral language had been the nearly universal and exceptionless practice for most of the Church's history, the sudden introduction of the vernacular—and until very recently, a bland and boorish vernacular at that—contributed to this serpentine leveling as well. *Ad orientem*, use of Latin and plainchant, and kneeling for Communion are simple but potent ways to remind ourselves that we are *not* "on a level playing field" with God, that

---

[33] Clayton, "The Smoke of Satan Enters From the West…at Our Invitation."

He is truly Almighty and Pantocrator, and we are His creatures and His subjects. These traditional practices effectively repudiate the aberration of democratic horizontalism that has afflicted not only our entire social life as citizens but also, for more than half a century, the Church's social life, that is, her liturgy.[34]

The dismantling of these things—the removal of Communion rails, the introduction of Communion in the hand while standing in line (again, I speak in reference to the Western experience as it developed over the second millennium), the disappearance of the acolyte with the paten, and so forth—is consistent with the overall warping of the act of worship into an act of precipitous self-esteem, one that is disturbingly reminiscent of the scenario played out in the Garden of Eden, where Adam and Eve looked downward and inward, away from God, away from the world that had been gifted to them, and into their own vanity and pride; seeking a self-affirmation that resulted in their catastrophic alienation from God, from each other, and from their very selves. For these reasons, I concur with Martin Mosebach's assessment:

> The Missal of Paul VI did not . . . prescribe the turning-around of the altars—that is the most palpably felt transgression against the tradition of prayer in the whole world. The priest should turn

34 See chapters 3, 7, and 9 in my book *Turned Around.*

> himself, along with the congregation, to the Crucified and to the Christ who will return from the east; he should direct his prayers, in common with the congregation, to the altar and to Christ. This change in the direction of prayer has caused greater harm in Europe and America than all of the relativizing, demythologizing, and humanizing theologies put together. It became patently clear to even the simple faithful that the prayers were directed, not to God, but rather to the congregation, which was to be put in the correct mood so as to celebrate *itself* as the "people of God."[35]

Contrary to a steady stream of progressive propaganda starting in about 1960, the Mass is not first and foremost a "communal gathering"—for there are many sorts of communal gatherings that are not Masses, and as the Church has consistently taught, a Mass celebrated by only a priest and a server, or in a case of necessity by a priest alone, with no congregation in sight, is still every bit as true and proper a Mass as one offered in St. Peter's Basilica with tens of thousands of faithful in attendance: each is the supreme sacrifice of Christ offered by and for the Church, His Mystical Body. For the essence of the Mass is *not* the circle of people who may or may not gather around the table, but the all-pleasing immolation of the spotless Lamb who takes away

35 Mosebach, *Subversive Catholicism*, 80.

the sins of the world: the sacrifice of Jesus Christ on Calvary, made present anew in the immolation of the Victim under the species of bread and wine, offered as a sweet-smelling oblation to the Father. Consequently, the Mass is a *theocentric* prayer: it is ordered *to God.* It is done, in the words of the *Gloria*, "*propter magnam gloriam tuam*" ("for the sake of Thy great glory"); in the words of the doxology at the end of the Canon, "All glory and honor are Thine, Almighty Father . . ." Yes, the Mass was given to us by Our Lord at the Last Supper for *our* benefit (since God does not benefit from our good actions!), but it benefits us precisely by ordering us to God first, giving Him the primacy that is His by nature and by conquest. We are benefited by being subordinated to God, yielding ourselves to Him as a rational sacrifice;[36] we profit from being decentered on ourselves and recentered on Him, our first beginning and last end. We stand to gain the most when we lose ourselves the most in Him.[37] *Convertimini ad me, et salvi eritis, omnes fines terrae, quia ego Deus, et non est alius.* "Turn to me and be saved, all the ends of the earth! For I am God, and there is no other."[38]

It is exactly for these reasons that celebration of the Mass *versus populum* or "facing the people" is not merely an unfortunate aberration based on poor scholarship

---

36 See Rom. 12:1.

37 This is the theme of my book *The Ecstasy of Love in the Thought of St. Thomas Aquinas.*

38 Is 45:22 RSVCE.

and democratic habits of thought endemic to modern Westerners; it is a contradiction of the essence of the Mass and a distortion of the right relationship of man to God. Because of its inversion of the worshiping community's proper directionality (including the priest's) to the uncreated Font and Origin, it functions as a sort of "immunization" against the rational self-sacrifice that turns our souls and our bodies toward the Father, in union with His beloved Son, whose meat is to do the Father's will, not His own as a man.[39] This directional inversion substitutes a Protestant notion of worship for a Catholic one. Erik Tonning summarizes the critique made by the poet David Jones:

> The reform played down the role of the priest as *sacerdos*, and the specifically cultic, sacral elements of propitiatory sacrifice, in order to cater to an ultimately Protestant-Humanist understanding of the liturgy as commemorative meal focused around preaching and imparting useful moral lessons.[40]

As Fr. John Hunwicke—himself a former Anglican cleric—explains:

> The sort of liturgical culture which Catholics have experienced since the 1960s is in fact a culture which

[39] See John 4:34 and John 6:38; see also chapter 4 of my book *Turned Around.*

[40] See Shaw, *Latin Mass and the Intellectuals*, 315.

was common in English Protestant Non-Conformity for many generations before the 1960s; and in a Protestant ethos it represents the theologically right and appropriate liturgical expectation. If the faith-feeling, *fiducia*, is the salvific reality to which the Christian must cling, then worship can have no other purpose than to produce and sustain it. It is not for nothing that Protestant ideologues have seen the Sacraments—on the rare occasions when they celebrate them—as merely "enacted Words." The problem for us is that for half a century most Catholics have been indoctrinated into that same essentially Protestant presupposition. When, now, they are exposed to something as ancient and authentic as *versus Orientem*, they can feel excluded by the celebrant—"Why isn't he attending to *me*?": the reaction of the toddler whose mother seems now to be devoting to the new baby all the love and attention upon which previously that toddler had an exclusive claim. "Leave your horrid private God alone and turn round and be my friend again." These poor layfolk are bound to feel repulsed; the outrage done to their gut-instincts may even make them revolted.[41]

---

41 Hunwicke, "Facing the Mystery."

In the pointed words of Fr. John Zuhlsdorf: "If your life is centered on Christ, you would more than likely be offended to see a priest turn his back to *Him*. If, on the other hand, you are centered on yourself, you would be offended to see a priest turn his back to *you.*"[42]

---

[42] Zuhlsdorf, "More on liberal liturgists' attacks."

Emphasis or Distortion?

"But wait a minute," interrupts an objector. "Let's say, for the sake of argument, that eastward orientation is better—that it is more traditional and more theologically meaningful. But isn't it also true that Mass is a meal, like the Last Supper where it originated, in which we receive the Lord as food for the journey, and that emphasizing this side of the reality isn't false and can even be a good idea sometimes?" The objection, in other words, is that if there are a pair of truths, one of which has greater weight than the other, nevertheless the one does not cancel out the other: both deserve to be brought to the attention of the faithful. Might it not have been useful, after so many centuries of a mysterious, transcendent form of worship, to "flip things around" in order to make manifest the *other* side of the Mass?

The objection is well-intentioned, though deficient in historical basis.[43] My answer: to privilege a partial,

---

[43] I will not give much attention here to the claim that the Last Supper was a *"versus populum"* affair and thereby justifies having the priest face the people. Ancient Mediterranean and Jewish banqueting customs make it virtually impossible to see the Last Supper as having been conducted either *versus populum* or *ad orientem*, at least in the literal sense of the terms. It was a *sui generis* Passover meal trans-

secondary truth over the more fundamental truth is to inculcate untruth. We can see this if we look at the history of Christian heresy. When the Arians privileged the truth that the Son is in some sense less than the Father[44] but neglected the more fundamental truth that He is God—God from God, Light from Light, true God from true God—they inculcated an untruth; for the Son is not less than the Father simply speaking. When the Pelagians privileged the truth that man is not saved without his own effort but neglected the more fundamental truth that even our efforts are God's gift and that without His aid we can do nothing, they inculcated an untruth; for we are not saved by works, simply speaking. When the Protestants privileged the truth that Jesus Christ is our Savior but neglected the truth that He saves us in and through a visible body, the Church, of which we must become members in order to benefit from His saving action, they inculcated an untruth; for there is no salvation outside of the body of the Savior. A subjective conviction that "I am saved" has nothing to do with what we see happening in the New Testament, let alone the history of the early Church. When modern-day liberals privilege the truth that man has innate dignity but neglect the truth that

formed into the kernel of a sacramental sacrifice; it was never taken as a simple model for Christian liturgy until the time of the Protestant reformers. For more on this point, see Kwasniewski, *Illusions of Reform,* 123–33.

44 See John 14:28.

his dignity is not absolute or independent of his social nature, with its ensuing obligations toward society and its susceptibility to just punishment up to and including death, they inculcate an untruth; for neither death nor the sovereignty of civil authority is contrary to human dignity, simply speaking.

In all of these examples (and they could easily be multiplied), we see how the emphasis of a partial truth, taken out of the context of the network of truths that gives it meaning, results in the establishment of a false system of belief, an "–ism" that separates itself from Catholicism.

The same is true of *versus populum.* When liturgical reformers privileged the idea of a communal gathering for table fellowship, but neglected the more fundamental truth (recognized as *de fide* dogma by Trent) that the Mass is the unbloody re-presentation of the bloody Sacrifice of the Cross, they inculcated an untruth; for the Mass is not first and foremost a group doing something together, but Jesus Christ offering Himself in sacrifice and granting us the opportunity to unite ourselves to this perfect, all-sufficient offering, the very cause of our salvation. It is the man who, over his lifetime, has become one with Jesus on the Cross who will be saved, not the man who gets together with friends to reminisce about the itinerant preacher of kindness from Nazareth. The emphasis of a partial truth (the Mass is a social or communal event involving edible refreshment), when taken out of the context of the larger dogma that gives this event its meaning and power (the Mass is the sacrifice of Christ, Head and members), falsifies the partial truth and in fact makes it to be harmful, in the same way as Arianism, Pelagianism, Protestantism, and Liberalism are harmful, although each is built upon a truth.

Celebration of the Eucharistic liturgy facing the people necessarily decontextualizes and falsifies the social nature of the Mass and unavoidably (even when the celebrant has a different subjective intention) suppresses its theocentric essence. For this reason, it inculcates a false understanding of the Mass, effectively *decatechizing* the faithful as to its true nature. It does not simply tilt the emphasis to one side or the other; it cancels out the orientation that is demanded by the holy sacrifice, which is to be offered to God alone, by a priest authorized to do so on behalf of the people. God alone, moreover, deserves and demands our adoration, and if it is not *clear* that we are united together in adoration of the One who alone is worthy of *latreia* (divine worship), then the unique right of God to such worship in spirit and in truth has been compromised or canceled out.

If we recall that for St. Thomas Aquinas, "religion" names the moral virtue by which we offer to God what is owed to Him by means of external signs and rites,[45] it would be accurate to say that worship *ad orientem*

[45] See *Summa Theologiæ* II–II, Q. 81.

and celebration *versus populum* are the expression of different "religions," at least in the sense that something different is being displayed and given by the human actors. The problem, then, is not merely that the practice of celebrating Mass "toward the people" has no foundation in the history of Catholic or Orthodox worship. No, it is much worse than an unfortunate sociological aberration, like the current fashion of body piercing. The use of *versus populum* erodes and corrupts the faith of the people as to the very essence of the Mass and the adoration owed to God for His great glory, since it takes away the most intuitive visual sign of God's primacy over man, and with its loss comes a severe weakening of the perception of man's duty to subordinate himself to God—in opposition to the ancient sophists and enlightened moderns who believe that "man is the measure of all things."

Clearing Up a Misunderstanding

I once received a forthright letter from a priest who argued strenuously against the position I have been explaining and defending. He wrote:

> May I ask a simple question? Where is God? Up there, out there? Or with us, among us?
>
> I imagine everyone would say he is both, he is everywhere, but clearly no arrangement of physical space in our churches or other buildings can adequately convey both his immanence and his transcendence. Seeing, however, that after centuries of *ad orientem* worship, emphasising the apartness, remoteness and unapproachable glory of God, the Christian churches seem to be in continual decline, many would contend that it is high time to redress this distorted balance and emphasise the presentness of God *with* us. This is what reformed liturgy seeks to do. It is, of course, a senseless caricature to see it as priest and people greeting or confronting each other in an anthropocentric way; rather it is priest and people gathering *together* around the altar which is the focus of our worship, knowing that God in Christ is present in our midst. If we

> can rediscover God among us we might be able to realise more appropriately his glorious apartness as well. It is not a matter of contradictory theologies, but of complementary ones. So far as I can see, we do not relate to God solely as an object of worship out there or up there, but also as a reality, a real presence in us and with us. Our symbolism cannot adequately convey all of this, so we make our choice of what we want to emphasise. Traditional worship has emphasised the glorious otherness of God; many now think we need to redress the balance towards his presence with us.
>
> The very earliest forms of eucharistic liturgy were, I believe, domestic. The book of Acts records the first followers of Christ breaking bread *in their homes.* It is surely highly unlikely that they would have set up anything like the medieval church with nave and sanctuary, and far more likely that they would have gathered at or around a simple table. If anything, the earliest eucharist was probably more like our reformed liturgy today than the grandiose *ad orientem* High Mass.

To his credit, this priest quite capably presents some of the main arguments used by critics of *ad orientem* and/or advocates of *versus populum.* Here is how I responded.

Dear Reverend Father,

I think this is the wrong way to go about the question. God is indeed everywhere. That doesn't help at all with determining how liturgy should be done. Starting from the simple fact of His omnipresence, we might end up with the attitude of religion-free hippies: "I worship God on the beach or in the mountains." And while it is never wrong to lift one's personal praises to God in the great outdoors, this is not the path any orthodox Christianity ever took for its weekly or daily memorial of the saving death of Jesus.

The question should rather be put this way: "What *symbols* do we use in Christian worship to express our relationship to God and His to us?" And to answer that question, we have to look to the three principles of cosmos, history, and mystery, as Ratzinger argues in *The Spirit of the Liturgy.*

The universe (*cosmos*), which is God's "First Book," gives us the rising sun from the east. That is why God's Second Book (i.e., Sacred Scripture) talks so much about the Orient. The sun, the moon, and the stars were given to men "for signs and seasons" (Gen 1:14). If they are signs, what are they signs of? We ignore nature at our peril—now, more than ever, when artifacts and technology insulate or even alienate us from reality. That the sun rises in the east signifies that Christ is the true light who enlightens every man (Jn 1:9).

Church *history*, for its part, gives us a consistent witness of oriented churches where the nave gives way to the sanctuary, which gives way to the altar. How likely is it that the custom of facing east to worship, which came into public view in basilicas across the entire civilized world as soon as Christianity was legalized in the early fourth century, was something made up on the spot? The ancient Christians were far too jealous of their customs. It is far more likely that their preferred manner of praying was rooted in the habits of prayer handed down from the Apostles themselves, as St. Basil the Great testified. To remain symbolically effective, eastward prayer does not need to be set within elaborate architecture or ritual, although clearly all later architecture and ceremonial is like the pearl that forms around this initial grain of sand.

Mystery, the third criterion, tells us that we should not worship in such a way that we risk deifying ourselves or our community. Our worship has to be outward and upward in order to reinforce in us through sensible signs that we cannot save ourselves but must seek salvation beyond ourselves. True though it is that the soul is the temple of the Blessed Trinity, it can be dangerous to shape public worship in terms of God's immanence within us, since fallen human beings tend to be self-absorbed and self-exalting.

Traditional forms of worship greatly accentuate both God's transcendence and His immanence: His transcendence, in the various ways already mentioned; His immanence by the fact that our worship is physical, sensuous, and concerns food and drink and other ordinary things, through which the infinite and eternal God meets us in a definite place and time. I have never found that a Latin Low Mass or High Mass interferes with my awareness that God is within; on the contrary, the traditional rite's wide-open spaces for prayer, intensive preparation for Holy Communion, and facilitation of quiet thanksgiving for the gift of Our Lord have greatly strengthened my interior life as well as my sense of wonder at the astonishing humility of a God who comes to dwell with us.

While a decline in numbers of Christian worshipers began in some places already in the middle of the twentieth century, it is a fact that the Catholic Church was booming throughout most of the world, with vocations, conversions, baptisms, and other statistics riding high. What happened? The increasing humanism of the twentieth century came to a head in the antinomianism of the 1960s,

> when progressivism, liberalism, and hedonism introduced profound unrest, malaise, and dissatisfaction with inherited forms of life and piety. But this was not the fault of the forms; it was the fault of those who rejected them in favor of sex, drugs, and rock 'n' roll—or, more innocently but no less fatally, felt banners, casual presidership, and folksy kindergarten churchsongs. The emphasis on God's "presentness"—"We are the People of God!"—coincided with the greatest exodus of Christians from public worship ever seen in the history of the world. If some reform was needed, what we got was certainly not it.

(I should mention that no reply was received from the priest.)

Temporary Expedients and Permanent Solutions

Years ago, the "Benedictine altar arrangement," named after Pope Benedict XVI, was all the rage in liturgically conservative circles. You have probably seen it: "the big six" (that is, six candles) and a crucifix are placed along the front edge of an altar, between the congregation and the celebrant, with the corpus on the crucifix facing the celebrant as a resting point for his gaze. Ratzinger's rationale was simple enough: the Mass is a transforming mystery through which we can come to grips with death and pass beyond it. The crucifix is central in worship, even as Calvary is central in salvation history. If, for whatever reason, we cannot or should not return to the *ad orientem* arrangement, we must at least face the cross together. In this way, the life-giving death of God is put before us. The candles, moreover, line the altar in a way that marks it off as a special place and helps us focus our attention on what transpires there, almost like lights that guide an airplane to a safe landing.

There was a time when I saw this set-up as a valid temporary solution to the dramatic pastoral crisis of the anthropocentric inversion of the Mass. Granting that it breaks up the closed circle and offers visual respite from the tête-à-tête, I can no longer see it as adequate to the magnitude of the *versus populum* error. The placement of six candles and a crucifix on the west side of the altar, though it may seem useful as an "instant fix," creates two major problems of its own. First, it leaves the false orientation intact, as the priest is *still* standing with his back to the east or to the apse that represents the east (and, in a church with a centrally located tabernacle, turns his back to the Lord!), and he is *still* facing the west which, as indicated in the Byzantine rite of baptism, symbolizes the kingdom of darkness. The idea of a "virtual east" represented by the crucifix, while clever, is too cerebral; it is contradicted by the "body language" of the sanctuary, the altar, and the priest. Second, this altar arrangement sets up an arbitrary barrier between the celebrant and the people, in a way that never happens in *ad orientem* worship, where everyone faces the same direction and feels the unity of this common orientation. In this way, it subtly accentuates the "priest *over against* people" mood that is already such an irritating characteristic of the Novus Ordo, which was composed by clericalists masquerading as populists.[46]

---

[46] I hasten to add that, as I have demonstrated in a widely read article ("The Normativity of *Ad Orientem* Worship"), the missal of the modern rite does *not* require *versus populum* celebration; indeed, it presupposes the *ad orientem* stance, which is a strictly separate question from whether the altar is against the wall or freestanding. See, too, Schrader, "'Altared' States." Regrettably, Paul VI set the tone for

I am not at all opposed to the existence of real, permanent barriers in a church whenever they make sense liturgically and ceremonially: the ancient curtains around the baldachin, the chancel screen or rood screen, the iconostasis, the Communion rail. Such barriers articulate liturgical space and provide for a meaningful progression of ministers and actions, while catechizing the faithful about hierarchy, sacredness, and eschatology. But introducing a line of furnishings on the western end of an altar in order to make up (somehow) for the lack of a proper common orientation is arbitrary. It looks temporary and temporizing, as it is, and more often than not, marks an awkward caesura in the sanctuary, like a divider between office cubicles. Interesting, from this point of view, is the poet Paul Claudel's protest against the denuding of experimental *versus populum* altars in France, as well as the problem of trying to load them up again:

> Naturally, as the convenience of the faithful [for "seeing the Mass"] was held up as the guiding principle, it was necessary to rid the aforementioned table of the "accessories" cluttering it up: not only the candlesticks and the vases of flowers, but the tabernacle! The very crucifix! The priest says his Mass in a

---

the implementation of the liturgical reform when he offered Mass *versus populum* in Rome on March 7, 1965: see Augustinus, "50th Anniversary of Paul VI's First Italian Mass."

> vacuum! When he invites the people to lift up their hearts and their eyes . . . to what [are they to look up]? There is nothing left in front of us to focus our minds on the Divine. If the candlesticks and crucifix were kept, [however,] the people would be even more excluded than in the old liturgy, because then not only the ceremony but the priest himself would be completely hidden from view.[47]

In *versus populum* is symbolized and promoted the anthropocentrism of modernity; its forgetfulness of God; its refusal to order all created reality to the uncreated source; its humanistic this-worldliness, which does not decisively subordinate the here and now to the Lord, the Orient, who has come and who will come again to judge the living and the dead. With this change alone, the liturgical ethos or consciousness of Christianity was shattered. We stopped facing God together and began looking at each other. If the old Mass were suddenly to be celebrated *versus populum*, in the manner in which the Novus Ordo generally is, it would be totally undermined by this one change; if the reformed Mass were to be celebrated *ad orientem*, this liturgical prodigal son would, by that *metanoia*, have already begun its journey back to the father's house.

---

[47] Claudel, "La Messe à l'envers" (written in 1955—which goes to show what busy beavers the liturgists already were before the Council!).

The eastward stance, with all that it symbolizes and implies, is not a mere accident, an incidental feature we can take or leave, like this or that style of chasuble. It is a constitutive element of the rite of the Holy Sacrifice. We should stop pretending that this is an instance of *de gustibus non disputandum*, where either "option" has something to be said for it. A Mass that refuses to orient itself in continuity with the universal tradition and theology of Christian worship is irregular and subversive—harmful to the priest and people whom it malforms in an anthropocentric mentality, harmful to the Mystical Body in which it perpetuates rupture and discontinuity, and less pleasing to God whom it deprives of due adoration. So much depends on the priest and the people facing east together that it is no exaggeration to say that orthodox Christianity will thrive where public prayer is thus offered and will suffer attrition wherever it has been abandoned. "Turn to him from whom you have deeply revolted, O people of Israel."[48]

May Christ, our true Light, the Orient and the Sun of Justice, who dawned on the world in His Incarnation and will return from the east as our Judge, grant each and all of us the grace to do our part in restoring this ancient tradition, *ut in omnibus glorificetur Deus*—that God may be glorified in all things.

48 Is 31:6 RSVCE.

Bibliography

Basil of Caesarea. *On the Holy Spirit.* Translated by Blomfield Jackson. Edited by Philip Schaff and Henry Wace. Nicene and Post-Nicene Fathers, Second Series, vol. 8. Buffalo, NY: Christian Literature Publishing Co., 1895. Revised and edited for New Advent by Kevin Kight, www.newadvent.org/fathers/3203.htm.

Claudel, Paul. "La Messe à l'envers." *Le Figaro*, January 23, 1955. Translation published at *Rorate Caeli*, July 28, 2017.

Clayton, David. "Connecting *Ad Orientem*, Sacred Art, and Ordered Environmentalism, Social Graces, and Hierarchical Society." *New Liturgical Movement*, April 10, 2018.

Clayton, David. "The Smoke of Satan Enters From the West…at Our Invitation." *New Liturgical Movement*, October 31, 2018.

Clayton, David. *The Way of Beauty: Liturgy, Education, and Inspiration for Family, School, and College.* Kettering, OH: Angelico Press, 2015.

Dix, Gregory. *The Shape of the Liturgy*. London: Continuum, 2005 (first published in 1945).

Hauke, Manfred. *Women in the Priesthood? A Systematic Analysis in the Light of the Order of Creation and Redemption.* San Francisco: Ignatius Press, 1988.

Hayden, Evagrius. "*Convertere, Israel, ad Dominum Deum Tuum*!: A Benedictine Monk Defends Worshiping Eastwards." New Liturgical Movement, November 16, 2015.

Hunwicke, John. "Facing the Mystery; or Catholic Crustaceans." *Fr. Hunwicke's Mutual Enrichment.* February 4, 2020.

Longenecker, Dwight. "From a Priest at the Altar." May 29, 2014. www.patheos.com/blogs/standingonmyhead/2014/05/from-a-priest-at-the-altar.html.

Magister, Francis. "What Attracts Homosexuals to the Priesthood?" *Crisis Magazine*, December 12, 2023.

Marini, Guido. "Clergy Conference in Rome: Address of Msgr. Guido Marini, Papal Master of Ceremonies." *New Liturgical Movement*, January 6, 2010.

Mosebach, Martin. *Subversive Catholicism: Papacy, Liturgy, Church.* Translated by Sebastian Condon and Graham Harrison. Brooklyn, NY: Angelico Press, 2019.

Oppenheimer, Daniel Augustine. "Towards the Second Coming: Facing the Liturgical East." *OnePeterFive*, May 20, 2015.

Pluth, Kathleen. "The First Step in Ecclesiastical Reform: Turn the Altars Around." *The Chant Café*, July 30, 2018.

Ratzinger, Joseph. *Milestones: Memoirs 1927-1977*. Translated by Erasmo Levia-Merikakis. San Francisco: Ignatius Press, 1988.

Ratzinger, Joseph. *The Spirit of the Liturgy*. Translated by John Saward. San Francisco: Ignatius Press, 2000.

Shaw, Joseph. *Latin Mass and the Intellectuals: Petitions to Save the Ancient Mass from 1966 to 2007*. Waterloo, ON: Arouca Press, 2023.

Shaw, Joseph. *The Liturgy, the Family, and the Crisis of Modernity. Essays of a Traditional Catholic*. Lincoln, NE: Os Justi Press, 2023.

Thurian, Max. "La Liturgie, contemplation du mystère." *Notitiae* 32 (1996): 690-97. Reprinted in English in *L'Osservatore Romano*, June 24, 1996.

Zuhlsdorf, John. "More on liberal liturgists' attacks on 'ad orientem' worship, bishops and priest who support it." *Fr. Z's Blog*, August 24, 2019.

Translations of the Bible Used in this Work

Unless otherwise noted, Scripture quotations are taken from the Douay Rheims Bible (DV), in the public domain.

Quotes from Saints and Popes on *Ad Orientem* Worship

"When our Lord died on the Cross, he was looking towards the west. So we pray facing east, as if to look at the face of the Crucified. And since he ascends above the heaven of heavens to the east, we, so to speak, accompany him as he ascends by our prayers and petitions. And finally, it is believed that he will come from the east in judgement: For as lightning cometh out of the east, and appeareth even into the west, so shall also the coming of the Son of man be."

—St. Robert Bellarmine

"It is also fitting to do this (eastwards) because of Christ, who is the light of the world, and is called the Orient."

—St. Thomas Aquinas

"We turn ourselves to the east to pray. Not that God may only be seen there, for he is everywhere, and is not limited to any particular place; but because our first home was in the east. I mean that dwelling that we had in Paradise, from which we were expelled—for God planted a paradise in Eden in the east."

—St. Gregory of Nyssa

"The common turning toward the east was not a 'celebration toward the wall'; it did not mean that the priest 'had his back to the people': the priest himself was not regarded as so important. For just as the congregation in the synagogue looked together toward Jerusalem, so in the Christian liturgy the congregation looked together 'toward the Lord.' . . . They did not close themselves into a circle; they did not gaze at one another; but as the pilgrim People of God they set off for the Oriens, for the Christ who comes to meet us. . . . [A]common turning to the east during the Eucharistic Prayer remains essential. This is not a case of something accidental, but of what is essential. Looking at the priest has no importance. What matters is looking together at the Lord."

—Joseph Ratzinger, *The Spirit of the Liturgy*, 80–81.

About the Author

Dr. Peter Kwasniewski taught theology, philosophy, music, and art history at various undergraduate and graduate institutions from 1998 to 2018, chiefly at the International Theological Institute in Austria and at Wyoming Catholic College in Lander, WY, which he helped establish. He is also a singer and composer who has directed choirs from 1994 to the present and whose sacred choral music has received performances around the world. Since 2018, he has dedicated himself to writing and speaking in defense of the traditional Catholic Faith, especially in its liturgical expressions. His books and articles have been published in at least twenty languages.